Includes Five SAT Words to Know

MEETS STATE AND NATIONAL STANDARDS

France

The Ooh-la-la Country Everyone Loves!

IT'S YOUR WORLD

LIVE • WORK • PLAY • LEARN

Where Do You Want to Go?

By Carole Marsh

Live • Work • Play • Learn

GALLOPADE INTERNATIONAL

Gallopade International is introducing SAT words that kids need to know in our books. The SAT words in this book have a gray box around them. Students can look up the definitions and increase their vocabulary. Happy Learning!

Gallopade is proud to be a member and supporter of these educational organizations and associations:

Association for the Study of African American Life and History
National Alliance of Black School Educators
American Booksellers Association
American Library Association
International Reading Association
National Association for Gifted Children
The National School Supply and Equipment Association
The National Council for the Social Studies
Museum Store Association
Association of Partners for Public Lands
Association of Booksellers for Children

At the time of publication, all websites referenced in this document were valid. However, due to the changing nature of the Internet, some addresses may change or the content become less relevant.

Other It's Your World Books

Africa: A Safari Through Its Amazing Nations!

Australia: The Land Down Under for Mates of All Ages!

Canada: The Maple Leaf Melting Pot Country!

China: A Great Wall Runs Thru It!

Egypt: An Ancient Land of Lore; a Modern Land of Oil and More!

France: The Ooh-La-La Country Everyone Loves!

Germany: The Country of Fairytale Castles and Cutting Edge Science!

Greece: A Volcanic Land of Ancient Olympic Origins!

India: Land of Six Senses and Intriguing Mystery!

Italy: The Country of Amazing Fountains and Awesome Arts!

Japan: An Island Country of Endless Intrigue!

Mexico: A Colorful Land of Exotic Culture!

Middle East: Ancient Countries of Current Events Headlines!

Russia: The Great Bear and Its Dramatic History!

South America: A Continent of Countries of Amazing Proportions!

United Kingdom: The Country of Ships, Sealing Wax, Cabbages, and Kings!

Other Carole Marsh Related Titles:

Mystery at the Eiffel Tower

French for Kids

La Table (say: la tahb-luh) of Contents

La Lettre (say: la leh-treh), A Letter from the Author

From the desk of CAROLE MARSH

Hey kids,

It's your world! It really, really is!
Of course, you already know that, don't you?
You surf the 'net, listen to satellite radio, watch television shows and movies set all around the
globe-kids today are much more "worldly" than in the past, and that's a good thing!

Now's a great time to learn something about another country–such as France. Why? Because
one day, you might actually visit there (if you have not already!). You might go to school there–
many colleges have ties with international schools around the globe. You might even go on to work
in a foreign country!

Many companies have positions in other countries. Companies are "going global" as fast as they
can. They have branch offices, manufacturing plants, and customer service centers scattered
around the globe!

So, ready or not: YOU are a Citizen of the World! And you'll want to be a good one.
How do you do that? You'll find out everything you can about that country, how it's the same,
and how it's different from your own country. What language is spoken there? What customs
do the people observe? What foods do they enjoy? What do they
do for fun? What has happened in this part of the world
and what is happening there now? It's fun ... and the more you
learn, the more you will enjoy whatever global opportunity comes
your way!

This book is a good place to start your learning journey–
so take advantage of the world– IT'S YOUR WORLD
after all ... and guess what? It's a BIG world,
after all!

Happy traveling and learning,

Carole Marsh
Always with passport in hand!

Why Should We Care About France?

France is one of the most important countries in the world. This beautiful country is extremely popular with tourists from around the globe. Everyone wants to come and see the Eiffel Tower, Arc de Triomphe, Paris Opera House (and its phantom?), burial catacombs of human skulls, Cathedral of Notre Dame, beautiful fields of lavender, World War II historic sites, and so much more!

France is a vibrant nation, active in world affairs. It is Fashion Central for *haute couture* (fine clothing). It has some of the most amazing art museums and artwork in the world. And French food is among the best cuisine in the world!

One day, you might visit France to see an opera, study art at the Sorbonne, live in an apartment in Paris, sail on the French Riviera, or work for a French company. It could happen!

Write home about it!
What will your postcard from France say?

Top Fast France Facts!

Important facts to remember about the country of France:

- France is officially called *République Française*, The French Republic.
- France has a President and a Prime Minister.
- France is governed by its Declaration of the Rights of Man and of the Citizen.
- France is one of the major developed countries in the world, active in international matters, and the global economy. It is an ally of the United States and other nations.
- France is a founding member of the United Nations and the European Union.
- France has one of the top 10 largest economies of any nation.
- France has 82 million visitors a year—the most of any country!
- France is a nuclear power.
- The capital of France is Paris.
- The official language is French.
- The national motto is "Liberty, Equality, Fraternity."
- The national anthem is "*La Marseillaise.*"
- The currency used is the Euro (and the *franc*).

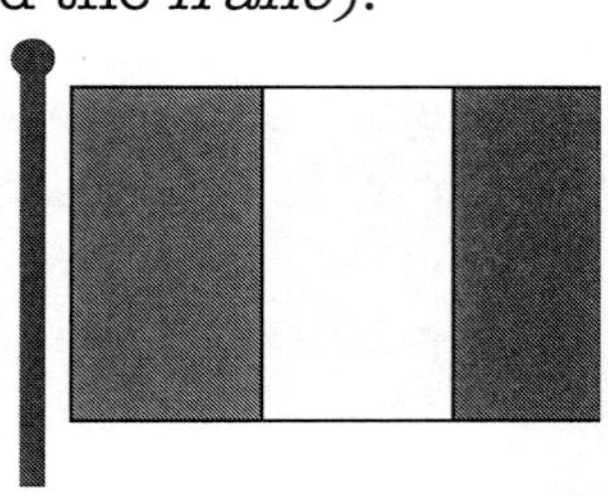

Now, you figure out the rest!

1.This is the French ____ ____ ____ ____.

2. This is the national ____ ____ ____ ____ ____ ____ of France.

3. *Liberté, Égalité, Fraternité* is the national ____ ____ ____ ____ ____.

4. The ____ ____ ____ ____ ____ ____ ____ ____ name of France is the République Française.

5. The _ _ _ _ _ _ _ _ _ _ of France is about 62 million people.

6. The name ____ ____ ____ ____ ____ ____ comes from the Latin Francia, which means "Land of the Franks."

Where in the World Is France?

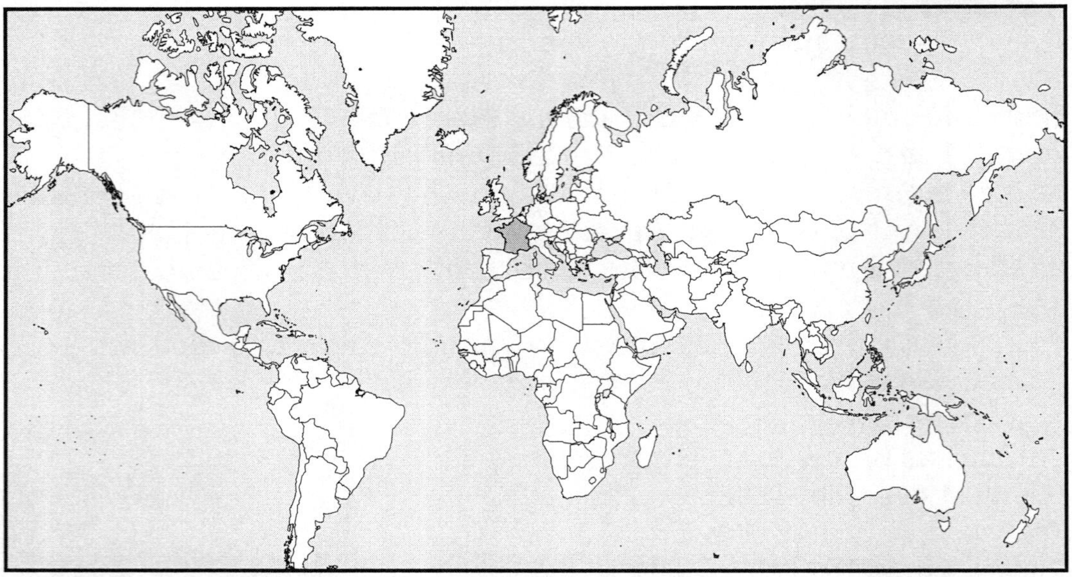

- France is located on the western edge of the continent of Europe.
- The nation of France also includes many overseas islands and territories on other continents.
- In Europe, France is bordered by the countries of Belgium, Luxembourg, Germany, Switzerland, Italy, Monaco, Andorra, and Spain.
- France is about the 40th largest country in the world.
- France is surrounded on two sides by water—the English Channel, Bay of Biscay, and the Mediterranean Sea.
- France is divided into 22 provinces.
- Major mountain ranges are the Alps, Massif Central, and Pyrenees.
- Major French rivers are the Loire, Garonne, Seine, and Rhone.
- France has a mostly temperate climate. Perhaps that's where the song "I love Paris in the Springtime...I Love Paris in the Fall" comes from?
- The hillsides of Provence in southern France provide flowers for the perfume industry.

Do You Know?

1. The shape of France most resembles:
   a. a Square   b. an Oval   c. a Triangle   d. a Hexagon

2. The highest point in France is *Mont Blanc*.
   Mont means: a. mountain   b. cliff   c. skyscraper
   Blanc means: a. black   b. white   c. brown

Kings and Queens! Lords and Ladies! Serfs and Peasants!

The Middle Ages were a turbulent time to live. During that era, kings ruled France. A feudal system let wealthy nobles "rent" land to "tenants" who would farm it and give a portion of the crops back to the noble. Children did not attend school, but worked the fields and helped with the younger children.

In 1337, England and France began the Hundred Years' War. English and French nobles fought because each wanted to be crowned King of France. A young girl, Joan of Arc, believed that it was France's divine right to win the war. Her faith inspired the French troops to victory.

Crosswords!

Use your new knowledge to fill in the crossword puzzle.

Across

2 Children did not attend __________, instead working in the fields or helping at home.

3 ____________ would rent farm land to tenants to grow crops and receive a portion of the crops grown on that land.

6 The __________ system is the system where one class of people own land and...

Down

1 _____________ inspired the French troops to win the Hundred Years' War. (3 words)

4 The Hundred Years' War was fought between France and _____________.

5 The _________ Ages were a very turbulent time for the people of France.

The Amazing History of France!

France has a long and dramatic history of kings and queens, bloody revolutions, and economic prosperity and prestige. Archaeological evidence shows humans lived in this area for at least 100,000 years. Early France was ruled by many different dynasties. During the Hundred Years' War, France fought with its neighbor, England. In 1348, bubonic plague killed 1/3 of the French people! After so many years of war and bloodshed, a young peasant girl, Joan of Arc, inspired the French people.

Joan of Arc

During the Renaissance period, France began to settle down but soon returned to fight a string of wars as well as a smallpox epidemic. France was still run by kings and in 1789, the people revolted against these rulers, desiring to govern themselves.

The French fought in World War I and II. Their leader Charles de Gaulle was respected for his role in helping win World War II, which had one of its greatest battles at Normandy.

Today, like many developed countries, France struggles with economic issues, the war on terrorism, immigration, health care, climate change, and other modern problems. In the meantime, it remains a beautiful country with hopes for a great future!

Timeline!
Number these events in the order that they took place, first to last.

_____ French fight in World War I.

_____ France fights with its neighbor, England.

_____ Joan of Arc inspires the French people.

_____ France experiences a smallpox epidemic.

_____ French fight in World War II.

_____ Bubonic plague kills 1/3 of the French people.

_____ The French people revolt against kings.

Famous French Folks!

Matching!

Match these famous French folks with their accomplishments.

______1. A philosopher and composer during the Enlightenment period in Europe, my ideas about government affected the French Revolution. My best-selling book led to the development of romanticism.

______2. A general in the French army, I later became the Emperor of France. I built a huge empire that included most of Western Europe. I set up state grammar schools, *lyces*, so that future soldiers would be smarter.

______3. A novelist and playwright, I am best known for a series of writings about life in France during and after Napoleon's reign. It is called *La Comédie Humaine*, The Human Comedy. I am a pioneer of realism, and my work still inspires writers today.

______4. A composer, I developed a style of music known as "impressionist." You may have heard one of my most famous piano pieces, *Clair de lune*, In the Moonlight.

______5. We are scientists who studied radioactivity. We won a Nobel Prize for physics when we isolated radium and polonium. One of us was the first French woman to become a physics professor at the prestigious Sorbonne.

______6. I designed and constructed the world's tallest building (at that time). Can you guess what it's called? Did you know it was meant to be a temporary structure? I also built a railway bridge that was the tallest one in the world for many years. And I designed the framework for the Statue of Liberty!

a. Honore de Balzac

b. Alexandre Gustave Eiffel

c. Napoleon Bonaparte

d. Marie and Pierre Curie

e. Claude Achille Debussy

f. Jean-Jacques Rousseau

Guts and Glory French Style!

Mixed Up!
Match the paragraph to the word that the paragraph describes.

A. Thousands of people were beheaded during the French Revolution. Executions in France were public events. The whole town came to watch as criminals had their heads cut off with this machine. The blade weighed about 88 pounds and would cut off the head in less than a second.

B. It killed about 25 million people in Europe in the 1300s. That's about 1 out of every 3! It caused a fever, black spots on the chest, and big black lumps under the arms, on the neck, and at the top of the legs. Most people who got it died screaming in pain within a few days. It was finally discovered that fleas from rats were to blame. People still get it even today, but now there is medicine to cure it.

C. As Paris grew, cemeteries overflowed. There was no place left to bury the dead. No place, but here. The bones of six million Parisians are stacked in 300 km (that's 186.5 miles!) of tunnels under the city of Paris. A sign reads, "Stop! Here is the Empire of the Dead."

D. During the 100 Years' War, she led the fight against the English in France. She was burned at the stake and later attained sainthood.

E. This beautiful building has underground rooms filled with eerie stage props and a lake. It is rumored to be haunted. A book that later became a popular musical tells the story about a murderous ghost in love with a young actress. Maybe you've seen it!

CATACOMBS ____

____ **JOAN OF ARC**

BLACK PLAGUE ____

____ **PARIS OPERA HOUSE**

____ **THE GUILLOTINE**

French Artists Make a Great Impression!

But not at first! A new style of painting started in France in the late 19th century. A group of painters broke the traditional rules of painting by making a few changes. These painters wanted to paint outside, not inside a studio. They painted scenes of life around them, not scenes from history. They showed the way things actually looked to them—not perfect. They used bright colors, not the dark earth tones used in years past. But these pictures were so modern!

It was hard for some people to see the beauty in this new sort of painting. It was a special challenge for the judges at the Salon in Paris. The best artists had their work shown at the Salon, but judges chose which paintings to show. Some of the new pictures were chosen, and some were not.

These artists wanted people to see their new paintings, so they decided to have their own shows. A French art critic went to one of the shows and saw a painting by Claude Monet called, *Impression, Sunrise*. He wrote that these artists painted "impressions" with loose, inexact strokes and were finished. He called them Impressionists and the name stuck. More than 30 years passed before this new art was accepted. Today, Impressionist painting is the most appreciated of modern art.

Impress Me!

Get out your crayons. Remember to use bright colors full of light. Choose something you see every day and see if you can make an impression!

Marcel Marceau, Master of Silence!

He wore a white face, striped shirt, and tattered hat with a single red rose. He could speak three languages. But he told his stories without ever making a sound. Marcel Marceau was a master of silence. He is perhaps the world's most famous mime. When he was 5 years old, he saw a movie with Charlie Chaplin, a silent film star. He decided then to become a mime.

During World War II, he and his brother were in the French Underground. They helped children escape to safety in Switzerland. Then he served as an interpreter in the army. He gave his first big performance to 3,000 troops. After the war, he went to a school for dramatic art in Paris. He created his most famous mime character, Bip. In 1949, he started his own company and performed around the world. For many years, he had the only pantomime company in the world.

In 1959, he began his own school of pantomime in Paris. His hope was that by mentoring, he could ensure the future of miming. Unlike plays or books, the art of mime exists only in the moment. There is no way to write miming. Marcel worked on a "language" that could explain the mime to students. He won many awards for famous performances that spanned 60 years.

Write home about it!
Marcel Marceau didn't use words to express himself, but you do! Use the letters of Marcel Marceau's name to create as many words with three letters or more as you can.

MARCEL MARCEAU

________________	________________
________________	________________
________________	________________
________________	________________
________________	________________
________________	________________
________________	________________
________________	________________
________________	________________
________________	________________

The Eiffel Tower, A Site to See!

The **Eiffel Tower** was built for the 1889 International Exposition to mark the anniversary of the French Revolution. The government held a design competition for a suitable monument. The design of Gustave Eiffel was unanimously chosen from over 700 entries. The tower was under construction from 1887 to 1889.

Workers using only spades dug the foundation for the tower. Carts drawn by horses and steam locomotives hauled the rubble away. When it was completed, the tower was the tallest man-made structure in the world! The Eiffel Tower is one of the most striking pieces of architectural art in the world today and is internationally recognized as the symbol of Paris.

There are 20,000 light bulbs in the tower, 1,665 steps in the east pillar to the top, and the total weight of the tower is 10,100 tons!

The Eiffel Tower is open to the public every day of the year. Over 200 million people have visited the Eiffel Tower since it opened.

On the first platform is a branch of the post office. If you mail a postcard from there, it will be postmarked from the Eiffel Tower.

Hungry? There are restaurants on the first and second platforms of the Eiffel Tower.

Every 7 years, the Eiffel Tower is painted in 3 shades of brown. It takes approximately 60 tons of paint to complete the job!

Create your very own travel pamphlet.
Concentrate on an area that interests you. Perhaps you enjoyed learning about the people. Or maybe it was the monuments that interested you. Fold a piece of paper into three sections. This will give you six areas on which to put information.

Faux Pas! *(say FO PAH)*
Or OOPS! A false step, a social blunder.

Customs and culture vary widely from country to country. Sometimes they vary in different regions of the same country. Here are customs and cultural differences observed by the French!

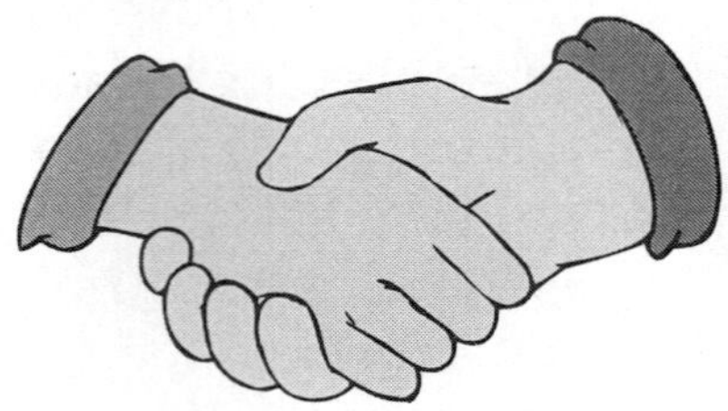

- The handshake is a common greeting.
- First names are reserved for family and close friends. Do not use someone's first name until invited to do so.
- Flowers should be given in odd numbers, but never unlucky 13!
- It is common to have a three-course lunch and take two hours to enjoy it!
- The fork is held in the left hand and the knife in the right. You hold them the opposite way!
- The French enjoy their free time. They work about eight hours less a week than Americans do.
- In the summer, many people in France take the entire month of July and August off from work or school to go on vacation.
- Dinner is the main event. Most people in France don't start dinner until 9 o'clock and take hours to enjoy it!

Create your own!

Customs and cultural activities can help define who we are. Think about your family and friends and come up with some new customs for everyone to try.

Parlez-vous Français?
(say PAR LAY VOO FRAHN SAY)
Do You Speak French?

The official language in France is French. French is one of the romance languages. In French, a noun is considered either feminine (la) or masculine (le).

Match it up!
Below are some common French phrases or words. See if you can match them to the English word.

Bleu	cat
Rouge	red
Le chat	good day
Le garçon	boy
Le bebe	blue
La porte	thank-you
La fleur	flower
L'avion	baby
Merci	airplane
Bonjour	door

Happy Holidays!

The French have 11 national holidays, including **Christmas** and **Bastille Day**. Some holidays may have a French twist!

Christmas is celebrated on December 25. Kids put shoes in front of the fireplace to be filled with gifts by Pere Noel! Wonder if those gifts smell funny? During the night, candy, fruit, and small toys are hung on the tree. Watch out for *Pere Fouettard*! He hands out spankings to children who were naughty!

Bastille Day is celebrated on July 14. Bastille Day celebrates the storming of a prison—the Bastille—in Paris. It is considered to be the start of the French Revolution and the birth of the French Republic. It is celebrated with parades and fireworks, a lot like the Fourth of July!

Write it down!
On the lines below, write a letter to Pere Noel. Tell him what you would like for Christmas. Think about how much can fit in your shoe. Also, convince him that you don't need a spanking, but maybe your little brother does!

France on the Stage and in Museums!

France has a deep culture of music and art. It is the birthplace of impressionism and home to many museums, including the Louvre in Paris.

2.

3.

Notes

1. The Mona Lisa is housed at the Louvre Museum in Paris.
2. Claude Monet, the father of impressionist painting, enjoyed painting water lilies.
3. *Les Miserables* is a famous book written by Victor Hugo and turned into a musical.
4. Folk music featuring the accordion is played in many regions of France.
5. The Paris Opera opened in 1875. People still enjoy the arts there today!

1.

5.

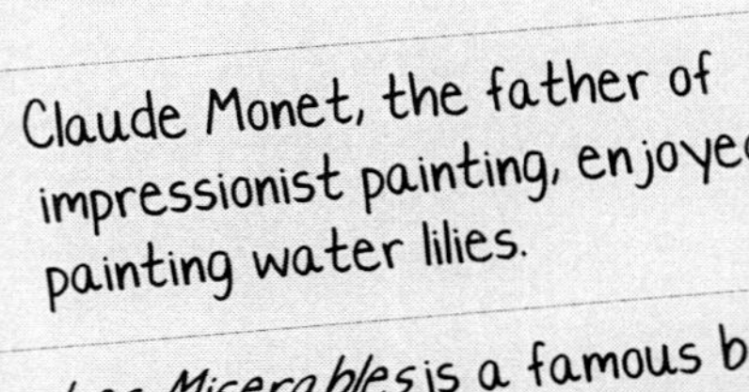

4.

French Fries Aren't French?

France is well known for its food. When people think of France, they think of food with rich sauces, breads, and cheese. You think of French fries and French toast, but are they French? Here are some common French dishes. Some of them may be made with ingredients you'd never dream of using, but that's what makes France unique.

Coq au vin is roasted rooster, mushrooms, and lardoons (salt pork) cooked in a wine sauce.

Foie Gras is the liver of a goose or duck. The goose or duck is fattened by force feeding it.

Frog legs are considered a delicacy in France. They are usually sautéed with butter, garlic, and parsley. Is this your idea of an unusual meal?

Crêpe suzette is a common French dessert. A *crêpe* (sort of like a pancake) is topped with a sauce of caramelized sugar, orange juice, orange peel, and a liqueur. The pastry is then *flambéed*. Step back! They just set that dessert on fire!

Bon Appétit! (literally, good appetite. Enjoy!)

RECIPE

Always ask an adult for help when cooking!

Chocolate Mousse

mmmmmmm...this was good!

INGREDIENTS

1 cup semisweet chocolate chips
5 tablespoons boiling water
4 eggs, separated

DIRECTIONS

Grind chocolate chips in a blender. Add boiling water and blend to melt the chocolate. Add egg yolks, one at a time, blending well after each. In a medium bowl, beat egg whites with electric mixer until stiff peaks form. Fold egg whites into chocolate mixture gently. Pour the mousse into small glasses. Chill in refrigerator until set.

Tour de France, A Race to Remember!

France holds the annual cycling race Tour de France, which takes place each July. The race covers 2,000 miles and lasts for 3 weeks. It is the world's largest spectator sport. The overall leader of this race wears a yellow jersey called the *maillot jaune*. The route changes each year, but the end of the race is always on the Champs Elysees in Paris. The racer who gets #13 is allowed to wear one number upside down!

Figure it out!

Figure out the answers to these questions about the Tour de France.

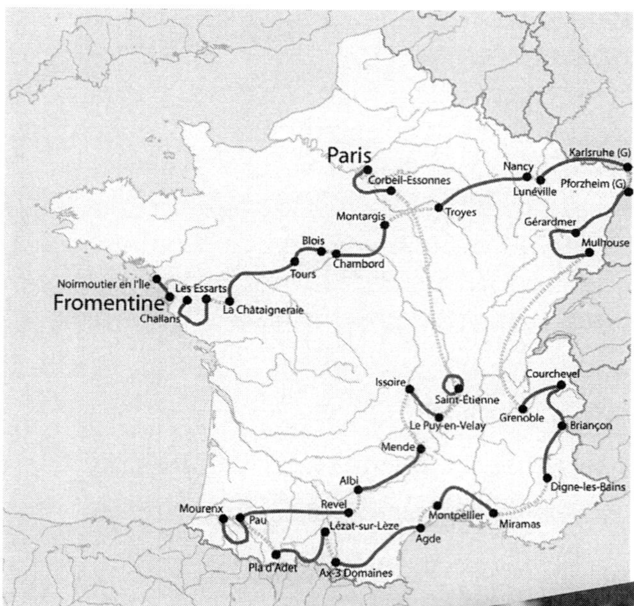

1. If the Tour de France is 2000 miles long and lasts for 21 days, how many miles per day must you ride in order to complete the race? (Round up to the nearest whole number)

   ____

2. One day's leg of the Tour de France is 96 miles. A water stop is set up at the halfway point. How many miles must you ride before you will stop for water?

   ____

American Lance Armstrong won the Tour de France a record-breaking seven consecutive years, from 1999 to 2005.

Did you know? France has hosted the Olympic games five times!

Paris...
City of Lights!

The capital city of France began as a small fishing village called Lutetia. Later it was conquered by the Romans and renamed Paris after the local Parisi tribe.

In the fifth century, Attila the Hun invaded Paris. It was said that the prayers of a young girl named Genevieve saved Paris from pillaging. Genevieve was declared the patron saint of Paris.

In 987, Hugues Capet became the king of France, and Paris became the capital city.

Today, the capital city of France is home to some of the world's finest art, fashion, and food. The River Seine is the heart of the city. All of the important buildings can be found along its banks.

The river divides the city into two areas, the Right Bank on the north and the Left Bank on the south. The Right Bank is known for its fine shopping. The Left Bank is known for artists and writers who lived there long ago.

Barges and *bateaux mouches*, large pleasure boats filled with tourists, parade up and down the river. The east side is where the ancient roots of the city lie. The west is home to the newer developments.

Why is Paris called the City of Lights? The "Lights" of Paris were the intellectual residents. They made Paris world-famous for culture. Artists, writers, and sculptors came to the city because of them. Today, light bulbs continue Paris' reputation. All of Paris—the fountains, monuments, and facades, stay lit until late at night!

Word Fun!

Place the Parisian Landmark in the correct Bank where it is located:

Eiffel Tower, Louvre, Champs Elysees, fine shopping, ancient roots of the city, Latin Quarter, Sorbonne, Pantheon, artists and writers, newer developments.

Left Bank	Right Bank
____________________	____________________
____________________	____________________
____________________	____________________
____________________	____________________
____________________	____________________
____________________	____________________

France Did It First!

Word Fun!

This is fun to do with someone else. Ask a friend for words to substitute for the blanks in the story. Their word substitutions will have a humorous effect when the resulting story is then read aloud.

I want to be the first person to ______________ (ACTION VERB) across ______________ (COUNTRY)! I've been training for this since ______________ (MONTH). I'm in ______________ (ADJECTIVE) shape. My ______________ (ADJECTIVE) adventure will begin on ______________ (FAVORITE HOLIDAY). I won't be hard to miss; I'll be the one wearing a ______________ (COLOR) ______________ (ARTICLE OF CLOTHING) and a pair of matching ______________ (FOOTWEAR). My faithful friends, ______________ (FAMOUS ATHLETE) and ______________ (CARTOON CHARACTER), will be there to cheer for me. I'm bringing my ______________ (NOUN) along for good luck. I'm confident I'll be the first!

On Pins and Needles!
French tailor and inventor Barthelemy Thimonnier invented the first functional sewing machine in 1830.

Can You Hear the Heartbeat?
The French inventor and physician Reneé Thophile Hyacinthe Lannec invented the stethoscope.

Get Your Motor Started!
The diesel engine was designed in France.

Reading with Your Fingers!
A Frenchman, Louis Braille, invented Braille. Braille is a system of dots that allows blind people to read.

Flying High!
Madame Thible, a French opera singer, was the first woman to make a balloon flight.

It's a Bird! It's a Plane!
In 1783, Jacques and Joseph Montgolfier sent up the first smoke-filled balloon. It was the first balloon flight.

Beauty Is in the Eye of the Beholder!
The Louvre in Paris was the first recognized art gallery in the world.

The Mysterious Prisoner
Mont Saint Michel, the Fortified Abbey

Legend says that in 709, the archangel Michael appeared to a local bishop and ordered him to build a chapel on top of a 258-foot-high mont. For 600 years, buildings were added, and added, and added! It was not easy. The rocky island overlooking the English Channel could only be reached by foot. Pilgrims came from far away to honor St. Michael. The monastery became a center of learning.

The island location made Mont Saint Michel a good location for a prison during the French Revolution. In 1815, Mathurin Bruneau returned from America and claimed to be the rightful heir to the throne of France. King Louis XVIII would not give up his crown so fast! He put Mathurin in prison at Mont Saint Michel. Mathurin wrote to his sister, the Duchess of Angoulême, to try to prove his identity. Only her brother would have been able to answer the questions that she sent back in her letter. He never received her letter and died after five years in prison there. Was he the real heir to the throne? We will never know. Today that letter can be seen in the National French Archives.

Word Fun!

Write 5 questions that could be used to prove your identity. Ask about facts that are not commonly known. We've given you an example to get you started.

Example: Where was I born?

1. ______________________________?

2. ______________________________?

3. ______________________________?

4. ______________________________?

5. ______________________________?

A Story of Friendship, The Statue of Liberty!

MY BFF!

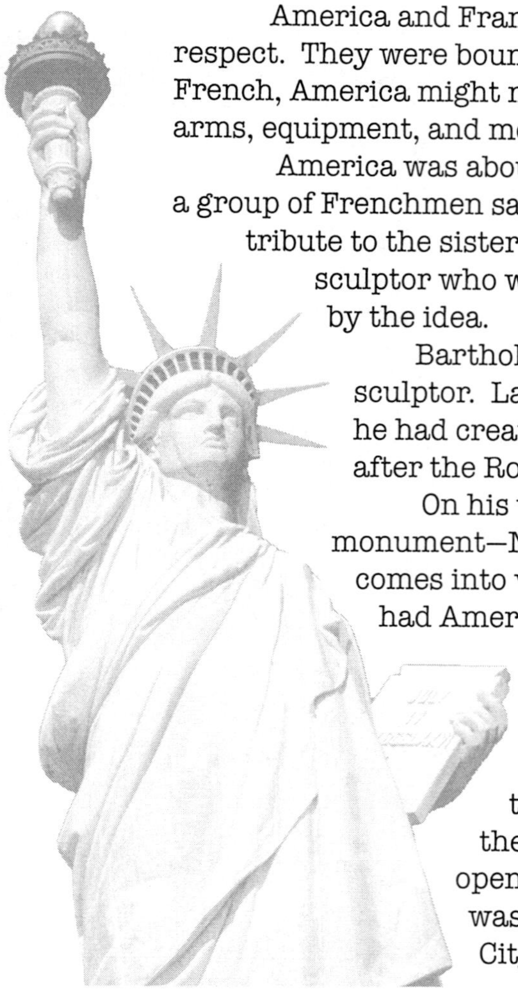

America and France were "two sisters" bound together in friendship and respect. They were bound by the dream of democracy. Without the help of the French, America might never have won its freedom. It was France who sent men, arms, equipment, and money to the colonies during the American Revolution.

America was about to celebrate 100 years of freedom in the late 1800s. As a group of Frenchmen sat around dinner, an idea was shared. A memorial to pay tribute to the sisters' shared dedication to liberty was suggested. A young sculptor who was at the party, Frederic-Auguste Bartholdi, was inspired by the idea.

Bartholdi had a passion for "large" art and a good reputation as a sculptor. Large public monuments were popular during this time, and he had created many of them. He decided to pattern the monument after the Roman goddess, Libertas, the symbol of freedom.

On his way to America, he saw the perfect place for the monument—New York Harbor, where the first glimpse of the New World comes into view. Bartholdi was charming and persuasive and soon had Americans agreeing to help with the monument. Americans would pay for the pedestal and France would pay for the statue. Fund-raising was difficult in both countries. But on a rainy day in October 1886, more than 1 million people lined the streets of New York in celebration of the statue. The day was declared a public holiday. As the parade went down the streets of New York, office boys opened windows and unreeled spools of ticker tape. The air was filled with curling streamers, and the people of New York City witnessed the very first ticker-tape parade!

Revealing Answer!

Follow the instructions to reveal where the Statue of Liberty is located.

1. Cross off the first and last letters.
2. Cross off any letter "O".
3. Cross off the letter that represents the Roman numeral 10.
4. Cross off the second "E" from the left.
5. Cross off the fifth letter from the right.
6. Cross off the seventh and last letters of the alphabet.

BEOZLXLOIS IGSEOLNANDF

Vive (say veev) la Révolution!
The French Revolution

The people of France were hungry in the late 1780s. The harvests were small and food was scarce. King Louis XVI taxed the people heavily. Anyone who spoke out against the king was put in prison. The monarchy, most especially the queen, Marie Antoinette, lived a life of luxury. They seemed to care very little about the suffering of the people. After being told the people had no bread, the queen was rumored to have said, "Let them eat cake!"

Soon the common people of France had had enough! They started to rebel, and by 1789, a *coup d'état*, a revolution, had begun. A meeting at the King's tennis courts ended with an oath to create a constitution for France. This became known as the Tennis Court Oath. This constitution would give the people an equal voice in the government of France.

Soon after, revolutionaries tore down the Bastille. This prison in Paris was a symbol of the king's power and violence. When he learned about the Bastille, King Louis asked an aid, "Is this a revolt?" The aid replied, "No, sire. It is a revolution!"

The people of France decided to get rid of the monarchy. The royal family was thrown into jail. King Louis XVI was tried for treason and executed on the *guillotine*, a machine for cutting off a person's head. Later, Marie Antoinette was also found guilty and beheaded.

Cross it off!

Starting with the first letter, cross off every other letter to reveal the name of the royal palace in which Marie Antoinette lived.

W V M E O R K S D A B I U L X L Q E P S

____

D-Day, Invasion at Normandy

Have you ever wondered what the D in D-Day stands for? In military terms, D-Day and H-Hour are used for the day and hour of a combat attack. Sometimes, the day and hour have not been set. Many times they must be kept a secret.

France was invaded by Germany during World War II. The Germans knew that France and her friends, called the Allies, would try to win France back from Germany. But how? And when?

The night before the invasion, Allied planes dropped bombs and thousands of paratroopers behind German lines. French Resistance forces fought the Germans.

American General Dwight D. Eisenhower commanded "Operation Overlord." On June 6, 1944, a huge army landed on five beaches in the Normandy area, located on the northwest coast of France.

American, British, and Canadian troops (156,000 men in all) were able to secure safe landing zones for more troops, and the Allies took back France. The victory at Normandy was a turning point in WWII and marked the beginning of the end for Germany.

Did you know?
In WWII the Allies were Britain, France, Canada, Australia, New Zealand, South Africa, Belgium, Holland, Norway, Greece, Poland, and the USA. In the Far East, China was an ally. The Axis countries were Germany, Italy, and Japan.

Figure it out!

List the countries who fought for the Allies and the Axis during World War II.

Allies

B ____________________

F ____________________

C ____________________

A ____________________

N ______ Z ____________

P ____________________

C ____________________

N ____________________

S ________ A __________

B ____________________

H ____________________

G ____________________

U ____________ S ______

Axis

J ____________________

G ____________________

I ____________________

Ooh, la, la! French Fashion

For many people, Paris is fashion. Paris is the home of *haute couture*, high fashion. The original couture garments are one-of-a-kind and designed by a select group of *haute couture* houses. The rules for being a couture house are strict. Many of the top designers are not included. Although very few people can actually purchase the originals, they provide inspiration for the clothes we wear.

The cost of these clothes is known only by women fortunate enough to buy them. There is no haute couture for men. Every garment is sewn by hand. Some pieces take up to 300 hours of work to complete. Only about 300 customers are thought to exist.

Couture houses include: Christian Dior, Pierre Cardin, Chanel, Christian Lacroix, Marcel Marongiu, Givenchy, Nina Ricci, and Yves Saint Laurent.

Figure it out!

A famous French fashion designer needs your help. Follow his instructions to help find the dress he is looking for to use in his fashion show.

1. The dress is not all white.
2. The dress I need has buttons.
3. The dress I designed does not have polka dots.
4. My dress would never have hearts on it!
5. I always put sleeves on my dresses.
6. I like flowers. The dress has flowers on it.
7. The dress does not have long sleeves.
8. I love ruffles! I designed it with three ruffles on the bottom.

Assorted Architecture!

Figure it out!

Use the following clues to figure out the name of this famous building in Paris, France.

- Construction of this building started in 1163, but it was not completed until roughly 180 years later in about 1345.
- Considered the religious center of the city of Paris.
- During the French Revolution, many of the sculptures and treasures in this church were destroyed.
- On May 28, 1804, Napoleon Bonaparte was crowned Emperor at this site.
- The Te Deum Mass took place in the cathedral to celebrate the liberation of Paris on August 26, 1944.
- An American university also known as "The Fighting Irish" in South Bend, Indiana, has the same name as this French landmark.

As They Say in France...

Here are a few French words you may already know. Why? Because we use them as "English" words all the time!

a la carte: with a separate price for each item on the menu

banquet: feast

bouillion: soup or broth (tiny, silver-wrapped cubes)

cafe: a coffee bar or small, inexpensive restaurant

camaraderie: friendship

carte blanche: unlimited authority

decadence: decay; rotten; falling down (usually means ideas or actions, not buildings)

déjà vu: already seen; that feeling of having seen or experienced something before

elegant: fancy, stylish

gourmet: a lover of fine food

Grand Prix: a type of motor racing, means "Grand Prize"

haute cuisine: a way of preparing food, means "upper cooking"

hors d'oeuvre: an appetizer

je-ne-sais-quoi: "I-don't-know-what"; indefinable something

joie de vivre: joy of life/living

milieu: the environment around you

mime: someone who communicates without speech

mousse: a chocolate dessert that is light and foamy

rendevous: a meeting

RSVP (répondez s'il vous plaî): please respond

soufflé: a dish (of cheese, for example) which you beat a lot of air into to make it light and fluffy

tromp l'oeil: make-believe; a sham

Further Resources

US Embassy in France
2, avenue Gabriel
Paris, France 75382
Cedex 08 Switchboard: +33 1 43 12 22 22
Fax: +33 1 42 66 97 83

United Nations
2 United Nations Plaza
New York, NY 10017

Paris Tourism
25, rue des Pyramides
Paris, France 75001

Normandy Tourism Board
14 rue Charles
Corbeau, France 27000
info@normandie-tourisme.org

Interesting Websites

http://www.tour-eiffel.fr

http://www.louvre.fr

http://www.notredamedeparis.fr/

http://www.paris.fr

Answer Key

Page 7
1. flag 2. emblem 3. motto 4. official
5. population 6. France

Page 8
1. d 2. a, b

Page 9

Page 10
6, 1, 3, 4, 7, 2, 5

Page 11
1. f 2. c 3. a 4. e 5. d 6. b

Page 12
the guillotine-A, black plague-B, catacombs-C, Joan of Arc-D, Paris Opera House-E

Page 17

Bleu	blue
Rouge	red
Le chat	cat
Le garçon	boy
Le bebe	baby
La porte	door
La fleur	flower
L'avion	airplane
Merci	thank-you
Bonjour	good day

Page 21
1. 96 miles
2. 48

Page 22

Left Bank	**Right Bank**
Eiffel Tower	Louvre
ancient roots of the city	Champs Elysees
Latin Quarter	fine shopping
Sorbonne	newer developments
Pantheon	
artists and writers	

Page 25
Ellis Island

Page 26
Versailles

Page 27

Allies	**Axis**
Britain	Japan
France	Germany
Canada	Italy
Australia	
New Zealand	
Poland	
Norway	
South Africa	
Belgium	
Holland	
Greece	
United States	
China	

Page 28

Page 29
Notre Dame